ENTRAINMENT

ENTRAINMENT
EWAN WHYTE

POEMS

EXILE
editions

Fiction, Poetry, Translation, Drama and Nonfiction

Library and Archives Canada Cataloguing in Publication

Whyte, Ewan, author
Entrainment : poems / Ewan Whyte.

Issued in print and electronic formats.
ISBN 978-1-55096-472-1 (paperback).--ISBN 978-1-55096-473-8 (epub).--
ISBN 978-1-55096-474-5 (mobi).--ISBN 978-1-55096-475-2 (pdf)

I. Title.

PS8645.H96E58 2015   C811'.6   C2015-903613-5
                                         C2015-903614-3

Text Design and Composition by Mishi Uroboros
Typeset in Bodoni SvtyTwo and Bembo fonts at Moons of Jupiter Studios

Published by Exile Editions Ltd ~ www.ExileEditions.com
144483 Southgate Road 14-GD, Holstein, Ontario, N0G 2A0
Printed and Bound in Canada in 2015, by Marquis Books

We gratefully acknowledge, for their support toward our publishing activities,
the Canada Council for the Arts, the Government of Canada through
the Canada Book Fund, the Ontario Arts Council,
and the Ontario Media Development Corporation.

Canadian sales: The Canadian Manda Group, 664 Annette Street,
Toronto ON M6S 2C8 www.mandagroup.com 416 516 0911

North American and international distribution, and U.S. sales:
Independent Publishers Group, 814 North Franklin Street,
Chicago IL 60610 www.ipgbook.com toll free: 1 800 888 4741

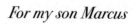

For my son Marcus

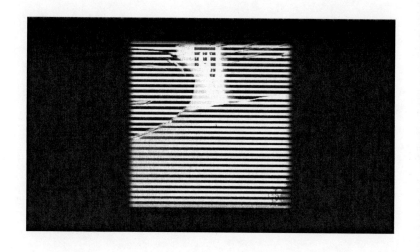

On a Yuan Temple Wall Painting in the Met

Diaphanous lines through blotches of faded colour,
the giant rising Buddha, tame behind the museum rail,

is still static joy within all former recognition.
The surrounding painted figures in procession

representing the constellations and order, juxtaposed
to the movement and noise of today's crowds

are reminders of the presence of ancient speech,
of elicited voices and the gesture of voice.

You are here, but your cosmos travels on, always
marching further away from us. Further through us

past colours and lines pointing to something
constantly here, still unlimited to fact.

Fioretti (of St. Francis)

A note about St. Francis who, as the story goes, was a rich dandy who partied it up in his youth. He was later very friendly to the poor and gave away his possessions so liberally his father disinherited him in the public square of Assisi. There he took off all his clothes so he would possess absolutely nothing, was given a burlap bag to cover himself by a member of the clergy and walked barefooted out of the town singing a French song.

Returning home
after an extravagant party

stopping for shelter
in a half-fallen country chapel

looking out over the fields
through the holes in the walls

he took off his rich clothes.
For a week he spoke with sister moon

and brother sun,
hearing their songs in inflected light.

After the last night at the first
moments of dawn

when the sun sends its sheets of fire
over the living surface of the earth

he woke with joy and shuddered
to the opening of the fields of flowers.

Fioretti-little flowers
There are references to *The Canticle of the Sun,* attributed to St. Francis
(but likely written a century later) lines 8 and 9 and to the 19th and early
20th century theologian Teilhard de Chardin, lines 13-14.

Catullus Poem 2

Sparrow, my Lesbia's pet
that she holds between her breasts
and lets flutter in her hands
and on her head laughing as he chirps
coming to her again and again,
she teases him with her fingertips
earning stinging pecks to her delight.
I wish I could dampen my desire
of her by playing with you, little sparrow.
I would dream of her naked smell
through your pecks to quench my miseries.

(C. 50, BCE.)

Bike Accident Poem

Bleeding and in pain,
some of my teeth on the road,
I am carried the short distance
to the hospital.

The beautiful women
on the street stare at me,
which is a delightful change,
except that I am covered with blood.

I realize I am going to live
as I can take no solace from
the emergency room kitsch, painted
waterfalls with a lone fisherman
standing in the water below.

My head is numb.
The nurses are lovely though,
they tease me for my art complaints.
I recite salty Catullus poems to them
while they pick gravel bits
out of my hands and face.

They laugh at his ancient words
through my voice, and that makes
me dream they are two mistresses
gently torturing the author of the poetry.

On a Night Bus

(1)

Travelling on a night bus between cities,
the overhead lights turned out,

a stillness of strangers resting side by side
in their seats.

Long after midnight, in the outer darkness,
along the sides of the highway

the mangled treetops of autumn pass
in a grotesque parade of shapes

against a half-moon haze.
While watching a procession

of collapsing monsters our ancestors
would have called gods,

I receive the confirming phone call
that you have died.

Most are asleep on this bus, from the back
I can hear the sleep-fighting voices

of talking children through the silencing
of their mothers.

In front a lit-up electronic device is reflecting
off a window

double-imaging the trees on the ceiling.

(2)

I think of you and your outrageous life
and its odd mixture of the high and low brow.

Your piano playing of Beethoven and Brahms,
your respectful mimicking

of Dinu Lipati's recording of Bach's Joy of Man's Desiring
during his remission from cancer.

Your rendering of Bach as a subtle question and answering,
and how you would obsess on the disembodied bliss of static time in art.

Your presence held back from the self-conscious rush to death we all face,
where there for brief moments is no time at all.

Against this, there were the hardened strippers you would date.
Bringing them into the church to drink wine

and play the organ after the Montreal bars closed.
Your comment that this urge against the sacrosanct

is in all of us to smash past an image to get to what is behind it
to find only other persona. You said you had grown tired of this.

Your weeklong bush walks of a hundred hundred miles.
Your interpretation of Colville's painting, Dog and Bridge,

the frozen instant of the dog crossing a bridge
where brooding imminence is created

by the carefully constructed geometrical design
drawing our line of sight to the German Sheppard in the centre right,

intensifying our sense of impending violence.
You spoke of the storms of sorrow that would come back on you—

the ordained demons of darkness
hovering near you. An aching loneliness that could only

be taken away by impersonal art.
Passing into a town the opposing traffic charges toward the bus

in a sudden pounding rush of blood.
I block the headlights, covering one eye, losing myself

in the central yellow line on the road.
After a time, I look up, waking into a changed landscape

to the sound of Mozart's Twinkle Twinkle Little Star
in the voices of small children from the back of the bus,

through their mother's gentle words about sleep.

Bag Woman Singing into a Carrot

Turning down the street,
past leering Louis's Coffee,

your songs a crosshatching to
talking pedestrians,

and street sounds. You are lovely
as always with your thickly

matted red hair, unwashed clothes
and cheap cloth hat

on the ground before you. You sing
cheesy Cyndi Lauper songs

a cappella into the large carrot you
hold as an imaginary microphone.

A group of teenage girls
sneer at you, but you sing on.

Every time I see you, I give you
some loose change, in thanks

for your cheerful presence
And also for your carrots

to which you have shown no mercy.

Bag Jesus on a Dirt Mound

On a thirty metre mound
of construction waste

he stands overlooking a highway
and passing sports crowds below,

singing incoherent word-shouts.
He is wound in see-through garbage bags,

the wrappings of plastic flutter off him,
a clothing of the appendages of flight.

His human-sized stray two-by-four cross is planted
in the ground before him.

He is a carrier of flight,
            an ecstatic bird man of sacrifice.

All day he is Jesus, offering his two-litre blood cola,
wine to the re-gathering gulls.

Heaving shouts of love and lifting his arms
to the slow cloud pocked blue, offering gestures

of clemency under its vault of hate.

Death at an Air Show

An antique World War II fighter turns
in the sky, spluttering across the haze-blue,

its cartoon-like anger sounds
falling steadily behind it.

Bland compared to the jets,
and the audience, swooning with delight

the more dangerous
the flight tricks become.

Is this what we, the crowd came for:
risk, a possible spectacle of death?

There is a feeling of excitement
in the paused silence before the event.

During a low altitude loop it seems
the vintage plane might not complete its circle.

The crowd roars between joy
and concerned alarm

at the flames flashing before
the impacting sound.

Ten minutes later everything continues
as if nothing happened.

There is an occasional announcement
on the loudspeakers.

"Emergency staff are attending to
the pilot."

A child in front of us asks her mother
if the pilot will be okay, before bursting into tears.

On Trying to Sit Alone on a Bus
or the Medusa of Caravaggio
(For Hisako)

Passengers enter the bus and sidle down the aisle,
Rather than share my seat on this intercity bus,

I try to look crazed so I can sit alone.
The beautiful women as usual pass and sit with others.

Staring at the distance bug-eyed, I try to match the expression
of Gericault's madman from an asylum painting.

A blank astronomer's stare pining into
an imagined foreground of emptiness.

I slip into thinking of the central condemned face
of Goya's "Execution on Principe Hill"—

a self-possessed gaze into a firing squad will get me
some solitude. I notice on the edge of my blurred stare,

a hideous passenger hovering between the two remaining
seats; I wish I could instantly drool to affirm my solitude.

After a minute's indecision he sits beside me;
I can smell alcohol through the stench of his body odour.

He is a transsexual incorporation of the Medusa of Caravaggio.
His blonde dreadlocks flopping around his shoulders,

his pallid expression of existential decapitation
a substance-inspired disembodied state.

He jerks his chest in a pre-vomit convulsion
with instant swallowing—

in five minutes, he is in an open mouthed snore.
The almost flapper-dressed woman sitting

in front us, turns back and laughs. In dread
I remember the Canadian Greyhound bus

passenger who sat down beside an unknown
rider before cutting off his head with a large

knife on a long stretch of country highway.
Still Medusa is there all through the night.

His reflected head in the window glass
is carried across harvested fields,

through scatterings of houses,
over forests up hills into the grey sky.

New Year's Geese on the Trans-Canada Highway

It is New Year's Eve on the Trans-Canada highway,
and it is snowing thick clumps of freezing rain.

The distance from every direction is touched
with a sense of immanent occurrence.

Later toward the city, along the sides of the road,
outer sprawl fights with countryside in intermittent bursts.

On one side, a freight train slowly passes with
sounding horn. For a time we seem sealed, still in falling

curtains of white, side by side to the sound of engines,
before the train inches ahead. Suddenly, above

they fly in low breaking formation, those deranged
southern fairground dwellers, mystical and honking.

In such a place only the unselected lost
of Darwin's labelling might surprise.

These birds that missed their time to head south—
their late attempt seems an inspired joke,

a Homeric attempt at a clownishly macho death.

Next Room

She called it a hate-fuck,
the young woman dying
in the next room.

We listened to her
when she felt
well enough to come out—

and tell us stories of her life
with Cystic Fibrosis.
Gordie thought she was almost

too pretty to die that summer.
She told us of her hate
when she was a child,

for those who would not play
with her, and for those who
would stay away from her

because she was going
to be dead in a few years.
And how when she was older

she would fuck them so they would
feel someone who was going to die soon.

She started with the teenage boys
she did not like, then men
in their twenties and thirties,

then much older men,
then her girl classmates.
She was twenty two

(but seemed younger).
She said she had done a cabbie
before going into the hospital,

an "older foreign man, I could not hate."
She would not talk much of her
ex-boyfriend who'd left her

for a healthy girl.
She seemed to have less hate
over the days she kept getting worse.

Her stories stopped.
One morning
she was not there.

She would say,
"I was always alone.
One day you will be alone."

Gorilla Cage in Riverdale Park

Someone says, "I wonder what this was?"
An older woman's voice from behind responds:

"This was the Gorilla Cage. My father
first took me here in 1969.

This was once the old city zoo."
Decrepit now, its concrete back wall

and front bars resemble a grown-over roman villa.
Even its covered roof is a sinister effigy of a home

with its cement imitation stonework,
fake windows and mock peristyle front.

Its joining chain is rusting through.
From a glance through its overgrowth it looks

like a sinister POW shrine
with the addition of a toy medieval

prison door. Inside, buckets, shovels,
broken flowerpots and garbage bags are now on display.

The late middle-aged woman sitting on a nearby
holding-wall (with someone who looks like

her teenage daughter) says:
"I don't think the ducks came here on their own."

(another voice asks:)
"Was it harsh for the gorillas?"

"Sometimes, the keepers used to torture them with noise
and sticks to get them to show their anger and power.

The little island you are now on would be so full
of people there was only room to stand."

"So the pond and bridge were here then?"

"Yes. Everything was pretty much as it is now,
but not overgrown. The patches of trees were not there,

and the zoo stretched out beyond this children's park
including the whole neighbouring block beyond the fence."

From the young trees beside the ravine paths
near the highway, and the scattered wildflowers

that now grow across the park,
it would be hard to guess what was once here.

Today, children's voices and red tulips open
among the trees at the sides of the long path

leading down to the pond, in scattered bursts
of open sunlight.

Landscape from the Back of a Train
    (an Alzheimer's visit)

My sight carries my imagination through
the kaleidoscopic distance

falling away from what was a moment ago.
Trees, bridges, water, and the changing

animal clouds in the sky shift with the
lights at the sides of the tracks

and overpasses that temporarily mark
all changing lines of sight.

After dark, the stars wander back and forth
over the top of the train through

leafless branches dragging Orion's feet
through the tops of the forest.

Later Sirius is running through the trees
shaking along the rails with my

imagination to the opposing train's
violent approach and passing.

A harbinger of anticipation of a coming
destination, a likely final meeting

in the consciousness of memory.
Its accidental forgetting,

its slow onslaught of senility,
changes the minutest memory of space

where the slightest breath of love is carried
away in the distance as though it had never existed.

An imagined place somewhere in oblivion,
where for brief moments, the fragmented

edges of recollection transform all things.

Guiraut Riquier: The Last Troubadour

How bleak must have been
the long dangerous journeys

between towns and courts
which gradually lost interest

in your elegant art.
Influenced from the east

but transformed by our medieval western
obsession with individual experience.

For us now, your world is utterly gone,
disappeared with the figures and colours

in the illuminations of your time.
Your mastery was widely imitated

before it slowly went unnoticed
in your lifetime. Your main audience

should have been the Gnostic Cathars
and Albigansians whose beliefs stretched

across Occitania (which became southern France),
into Spain, through northern Italy

into Bosnia and the Balkans.
They supported the early troubadours

and shared some of their values.
You were fourteen when their great

stronghold of Montsegur fell
in the final brutal crusade against them.

You would have heard living accounts
of how over two hundred Cathar Perfects

were burnt alive in an enormous fire
near the *prat des cramats* at the foot of the castle.

Of that war, Arnaud, the Cistercian abbot who was
a commander in the crusade, wrote to Pope Innocent the Third.

"Today your Holiness, twenty thousand heretics
were put to the sword, regardless of age, rank, or sex."

The older surviving Cathar sympathizers
were a large part of your audience.

They still admired the troubadours, but they
slowly died off and you lost your patrons

For a while you worked as a poet
for Almarich the Fourth,

Viscount of Narbonne, but you not fully recognized.
At forty you crossed the Pyrenees

and worked as a poet for Alfonso the Tenth
for ten years. After you re-crossed

the Pyrenees and wrote for Henry the Second
Count of Rodez, who gave troubadours protection.

But times had changed, court entertainers
could sing the poems and songs

of the troubadours and do juggling tricks as well.
Original troubadour poems had become superfluous

and you found no new patrons.
In the regional economic decline you moved back

to the town of your birth and found
employment writing religious poetry.

You could no longer write of latent mysticism
in the Gnostic language of god as all forms of love.

The world had changed. The Catholic Church
had won and dissent was no longer an option.

Jongleurs and minstrels called themselves
troubadours. And the troubadours were no more.

In your last known poem you wrote:

*"I remember my difficult past, I look at the merciless present,
and when I think of the future, I have true reason to weep.*

I will have to stop singing... for truly I came too late."

Lines in the Style of Tibullus

My dreaded birthday is coming again.
I will spend it in the distant country.
My friends are not here
to laugh with me.
There is a shallow lake
and empty woods
and a small cottage that would bore
an urban girl.

Sulpicia, you pester me too much—
travelling is rarely fun.
If you abduct me, my soul
and my heart shall remain here
though you say
you try to keep me
from them for my own good.

Istvan Kantor Takedown
(Notes toward an essay in poetry)

In a one-off extempore film, we see Kantor walking
inside the Hamburger Bahnhof Museum.

He moves slowly, though there is something calculating
about him. He looks quickly at contemporary and modern

works of art, before pausing in front of what resembles pieces
of oversized chopped cabbage on the floor. Gallery goers

pass talking in German. The security guards are close,
husky Teutons in the service of art. It is clear he is being

watched. At first glance, the paintings on the walls seem out
of place beside the contemporary work on the floor.

Kantor looks past the art and hovering guard staff searching
for something. The video narration records

the surroundings with occasional words by Kantor himself.
A number of rooms, of visitors, and art later we enter a large

open space interrupted by centred stairs flanked by handrails,
a sterile deliberately broken up space, with hallways on its sides

leading to other rooms. Above human height on a large flat wall
beneath the stairs, in large block letters is written in German,

"Beuys: We are the Revolution"

The guards stand by. And Kantor still wearing sunglasses
and sporting an ink X on the side of his head and almost

combat clothes in Monty Cansin persona. He walks under the text
of the ten or so metre long wall, turns his back to the stalking guard

and camera. He is slower than expected in trying to open a rolled sign
while turning to us and the camera. I find myself pleading

for the sign to open. Two guards are on him at once wrestling his sign
away. It is the almost pathetic struggling of a prisoner ushered to a scaffold.

We can hear Kantor's voice muffled then shouting,

"It's just a sign...
It's just a sign...
It's just a sign..."

mixed with foot scuffing sounds, he is pushed up the stairs but
slows to face the camera in mid-wrangle, saying firmly,

"We Are the Revolution"
"We Are the Revolution"
"We Are the Revolution."

His partly unfurled sign is crumpled in a hand of a guard.
What does it say?

He is shuffled off...Some gallery goers take photos.
What is this...this Neoism? Is this art?

Is there a feeling of the eternal in it?
An ecstatic joy or beauty, an instant

of transcendent wholeness,
which for a brief moment denies all sense of time?

Certainly there is a stifling of voice. And here, his art however
intentionally, underlines the impotence of revolution.

And for Kantor here, it seems the gesture of revolution is
the very essence of artistic expression.

It is an unconsciously religious posture,
his act of rebelling a secular shamanic ritual.

Here there is no end to achieve, it is
just an intervention to remind us to think of art as an almost living

entity, ultimately organic (in imaginative terms), joyfully impersonal
but fragile when framed in a museum setting.

The emptied room
is cold in its silence and stark words

"We are the Revolution"

Kantor's unread sign says "And so are we."

A Southern Ramble
(From a conversation with a local swinging a handgun)

"I just want you, dammed liberal, to know
that every night before I go to bed

I get down
on my hands and knees

and thank the Good Lord
for Smith & Wesson."

An Ibis Flies By

Out of nowhere, in the midst
of a conversation,

about a civil war battle a mile
up the road,

beside where local Georgia fisherman,
now tie up their boats,

Ibis flies by, low and graceful, with a long
stretched neck and ugly head.

watching us with one fixed eye
eases away in a gust of wind.

The old timer talking, says

"Bird's like a Yankee, not sure
if we want to eat him or not."

Graffiti for the Palatine

When here
humour the gods.

If questioned
blame them!

Antipsychotics an Afterthought
(a remembrance of a ramble by John B.)

"The alien gods are green
and descending from the sky.

Perhaps I should have told
my doctor I smoke a lot

before taking that prescription
stuff? Homer should have

written about this.
Well I guess he kinda did."

A Posthumous Visit

Peter's brother says to him at their mother's
graveside:

"Hey Peter I want to show you something."

"What?"
"Over here."

"This is a cemetery, we don't know anyone here."
"Just come on."

They walk onto a bridge.
"What kind of place is this?"

"It's where people who can't afford graves
cast the ashes of their relatives."

Peter looks at the little plaques on the rail
and says,

"This is a communal ash dump?"

Looking at the lush grass along the banks
of the little stream below he says,

"There's too much flora around here
for comfort."

"That must be where the ashes pile up.
Hell, it's as green as the Amazon."

"There must be bone chips down there,
when someone gets cremated,

it is not a thorough job, especially when
you're on a budget."

"At fifty-two with a prolepsis,
I'm next in line for this event.

When the city health department
takes the bridge down

my plaque will probably
end up in some cousin's

garage between a can of paint
and a license plate."

"Did you say something?"
"No, let's go."

Bird-Man of Lascaux

Suspended in air beside a dying bison's dance,
weapon and spear-thrower broken under your feet.

A staff with a bird's head points upward
away from the grasp of your downward reaching arms.

Your legs are straight, your own bird's head
with partially open beak

is tilted back, in trance or death.
Are you calling out as bearer of passage to another place?

The wounded bison faces you,
bleeding his life out through a broken spear in his side

his entrails spilling. In the stillness,
of seventeen-thousand-year-old blown paint,

you are still wrapped in a dance of death.
Calling out as a bird to the bison

to carry him to a sacred place, in thanks,
for his giving of his own flesh for your life?

Is the bison breathing on the corners
of your face bringing you back to dance

with him in death?
Or are you dead? Your erect penis faces the bison

as if to counter charge his horns opposing you.
Are your unheard sounds a clatter of voice

and life-giving rush of blood struggling to stay alive
but accepting of death as animals do with calm

or at its inevitable embrace? All over the cave humans
are drawn as stick creatures and nowhere else is there

a fully drawn human form. Compared to the hunted animals
we are insignificant. Their foregrounds of full volume,

of shape, and elegance of intended movement mythologize—
godlike power. Inside your body and in the body

of the bison and all around the animals in the cave
are ancient star-charts, painted constellations

you may have become or travelled to, voyaging through space,
accompanying the animal gods on their journeys.

Freama's Portfolio Bag

I bought your old leather portfolio bag
from a thrift store yesterday.

It must be 50 years old.
I hope you, its former owner, are still alive,

not that I have a personal
stake in the matter.

Your portfolio is well and in use,
some major re-stitching

has brought it back like Lazarus.
You left your school transcript

in one of the side pockets. I could not help
reading, its date of issue Oct 27, 1972.

It says you were born in 1940,
and entered the University of Manitoba in 1958.

I put it back in the side pocket.
and it continues to accompany your bag on its journeys.

It is a delightfully shocking document.
Your antipathy for math is most admirable.

On your first try with Algebra, Trigonometry
and Geometry, you scored 13%.

Improvement was on the way though,
the next year you improved to 26%,

before being awarded an F and a blank
on your third attempt in 1961.

On your fourth attempt in September 1962
you scored a 16% which is written above a line

that reads, *Failed Year -Permitted to repeat in error.*
The same year you scored 38%

in Introduction to Psychology.
You must be a person

with the persistence
of the horse in Orwell's *Animal Farm.*

The type of person a
drunken grandmother would like to give

hugs to for losing efforts.

You had one pass.
I wonder what went on

in your French class in 1960,
you scored 90%.

In Western Civilization that year you managed 45%.
In a History of Philosophy course you also scored 45%.

Before you were kicked out in the spring of '63, you gave
Algebra, Trigonometry and Geometry one more try.

In your fifth and final attempt you peaked at 29%.

O Freama, what Dog of Undergods
never awoke to your academic cause?

Or was there an awakening after your final expulsion?
Did you make one final return like a kitsch Hollywood hero?

There is no entry after this.
Fare you well wherever you may be.

Traffic Court: A Burlesque

The court recorder intones
like a TV preacher:

"We are all to rise
for the Justice of the Peace."

He arrives late for the appointed hour,
walking down the aisle of bad architecture

commensurate with his smirk.
I half expect to hear the recorder

announce the singing
of a routine hymn,

some nasty unmusical thing
of crime and its desserts.

The Parking Furies,
uniforms pressed, shoes shined,

sit in the front pew
like bully boys and girls

primped from the playground.
The prosecution, slowly, case by case

exposes our names and crimes
for all to hear:

"Parking on a curb"
"Parking in a loading zone"

"Parking on the wrong side of the street"
and fiendish "unpaid meters."

The prosecuting Virago,
complete with skinny legs

and power skirt (she no doubt
sports lingerie and a whip on weekends)

continues perfunctorily
while We, the terrible accused, wait

hoping for an intervening God.
Not unlike the descending Venus

when she, clouded
herself with invisibility,

coming from the sky to protect
her warrior son Aeneas

after he was struck by a boulder
on the battlefield of Troy

writing in pain,
but still wanting to fight.

A mist surrounded him,
he was snatched from death

by the arms of a goddess
and carried to a distant place.

No such luck around this prosecuting
Virago; she enjoys her job.

Finding it easier to be attrite than contrite
I ponder my embarrassing stomach flu excuse.

When the Virago calls my case
there is no hint of anything

beyond the ugly mundane.
She calls the name of my

assailing Fury.
Again she calls the Fury to be met with silence.

She sounds
as sad as the Argonauts

calling for the lost Hylas.
She looks back to the main door

before she says quietly,
"You're lucky today."

In the end, O deus ex machina
and happy dancing girls,

a hundred bucks saved for my next rent
for Nemesis, goddess of revenge

may have smiled from afar,

on that "parking fury"
with my ill-timed affliction.

A Swinger of Sorts

My neighbour, a two-metre tall ex-Mennonite
with a broken salad spinner, swings a tea-cloth

bullroarer for one from his front steps. He looks like
a stoned Viking hurling threats at a passing whale!

No local god or tree comes close to watch.
The tomatoes cut, the onions, garlic, and watercress

await the photosynthesis from the opening shroud.

I. V. Smokers

Outside hospital doors, usually under
No Smoking signs, they stand alone or sit smoking

in clusters, sometimes trying to go unnoticed in their
hospital gowns, wristbands and hats. I.V. bags hanging

like scarecrows at their sides, where the needles
link them to elixir flows

as they tolerate constant street pigeons'
familiar approaches, as though each were a secret lover.

Four Misheard Lines from Conversations

My heart feels like a fucked octopus.

You're about as hot as Jesus in lingerie.

C'est comme les mamales du Jesu.

I injured my prostate reading Proust.

Street Preacher on an Overpass

On the off-ramp of an overpass
lifted high over an opposing freeway

he stands above passing sports crowds below
wagging his tongue through holy phrases

in accidental parody of his modelled hero,
he pauses now and then, perhaps trying to think

of something profound to say, before he
continues with his garbled "TV preacher" style epithets—

but it is just the gesture of his elevated form
in space which is the essence of a monumental

religious act. His word shouts are merely
an explanation of his body's presence.

His crazed throat sounds,
the thunderclap following far behind.

ACKNOWLEDGEMENTS

Hisako Omori, Barry Callaghan, Michael Callaghan,
Raza Rizvi, Kelley Baker, Christine Tremblay, Sean Lipsett,
Dan Larabie, Patrick Georges, Mark Robertson, Mike Kirney,
Bonnie Bowman, Siobhan Flanagan, Peter Cresswell,
Art Szombathy, Peter De Sotto, Mark Achbar, Laurie Kwasnik,
Richard Kopycinski, Steve Davies, Evelyn K., Eve K.,
Shannon G., Britta Hardes, Peter Jermyn, Viktor Mitic,
Blair Walker, Bald Bruce Jones, Jason Logan, Tamir Baron,
N. Vasovic, Sasha Wentges, Peter Faz, Kurt Weider,
Molly Peacock, Tomasz Rózycki. Goran Simic, James Arthur,
Joe Duffy, Arthur Ulamek, Jeph Nightingale, J.Perry,
Howard Goldstein, Siobhan Jamison, Maria Coletsis,
Jose Tomaz, Darrick Weibe, John and Helen Fell,
Christina Starr, Monty Cansin, Vladimir Azarov.

Ashley Ohman for the photograph of her video work,
Coldbeat, on pages xi and 49.

I thank the Ontario Arts Council
for providing me with a Writers Reserve grant
toward this project.

Some of these poems have been published in the following;
Descant, Literary Review of Canada, Exile: The Literary Quarterly, Encore, Maisonneuve, Poeisis *Journal of the Arts, The Acrobat, Toronto Quarterly, Seraphim, Mostavi* (Belgrade), *Koraci* (Serbia) *Garden Variety* (Anthology), *Steel Bananas* (Anthology), *Scarborough Art Book,* and *Ottawatter.*